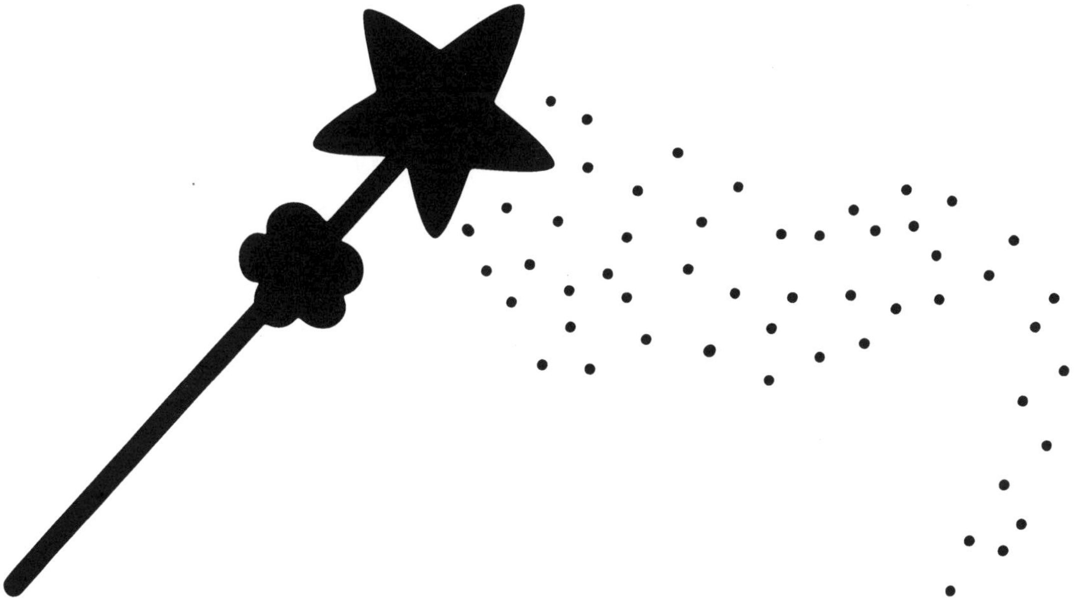

This notebook belongs to:

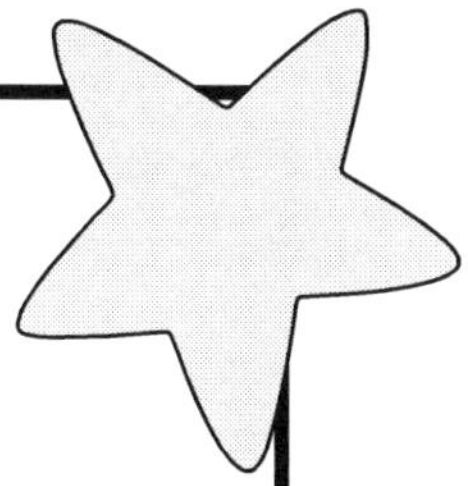

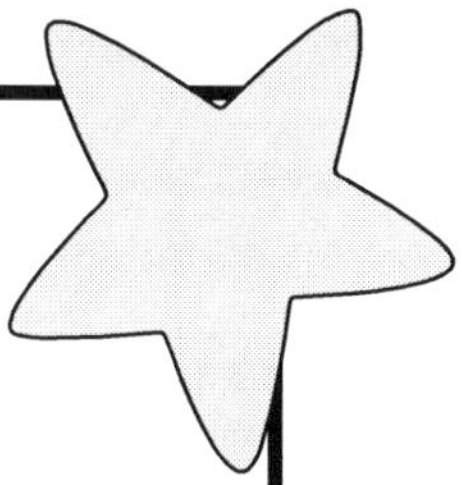

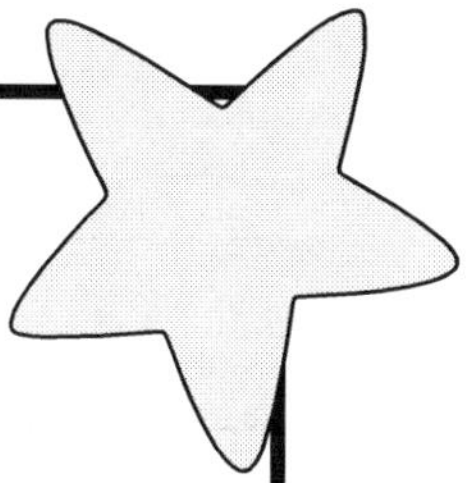

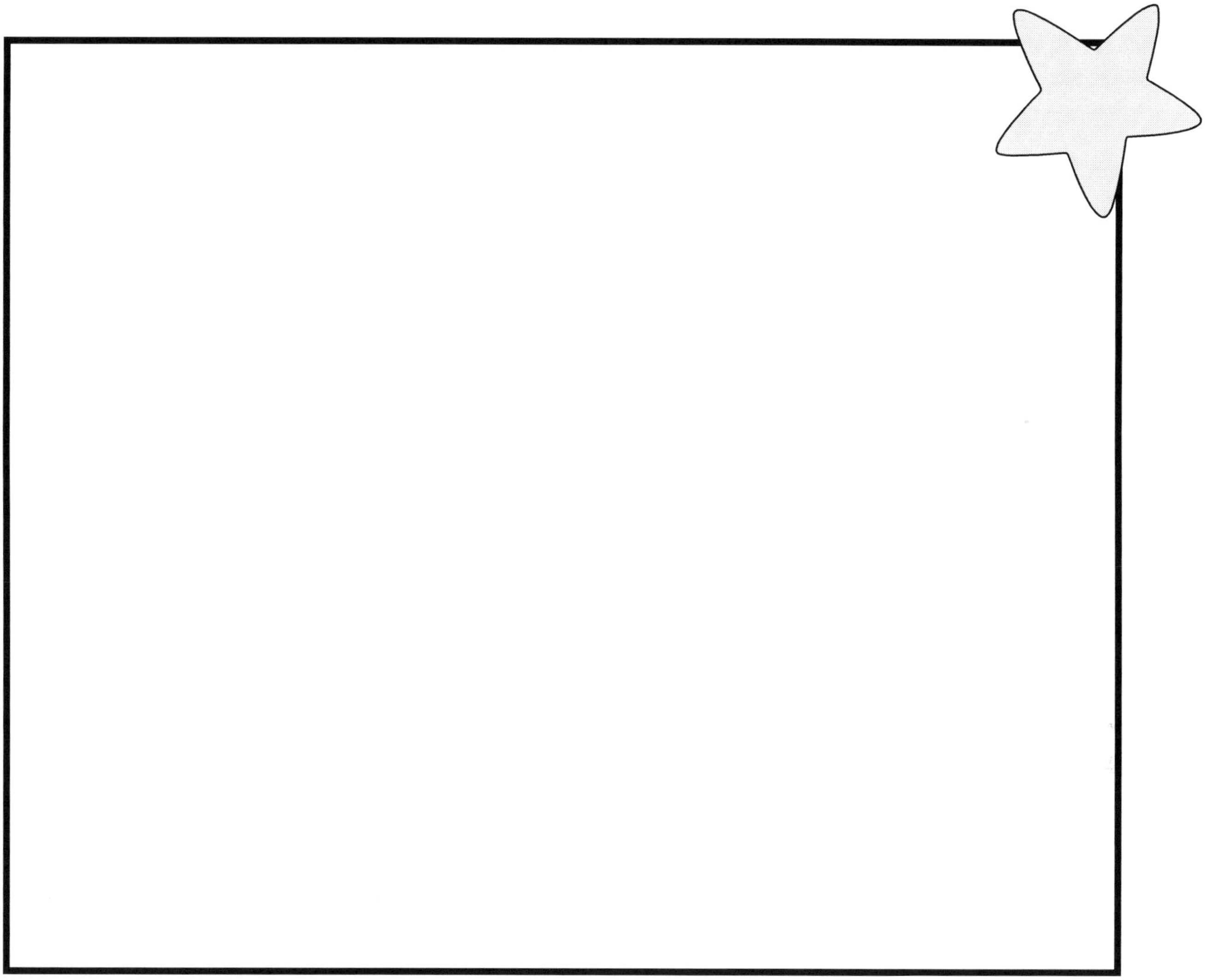

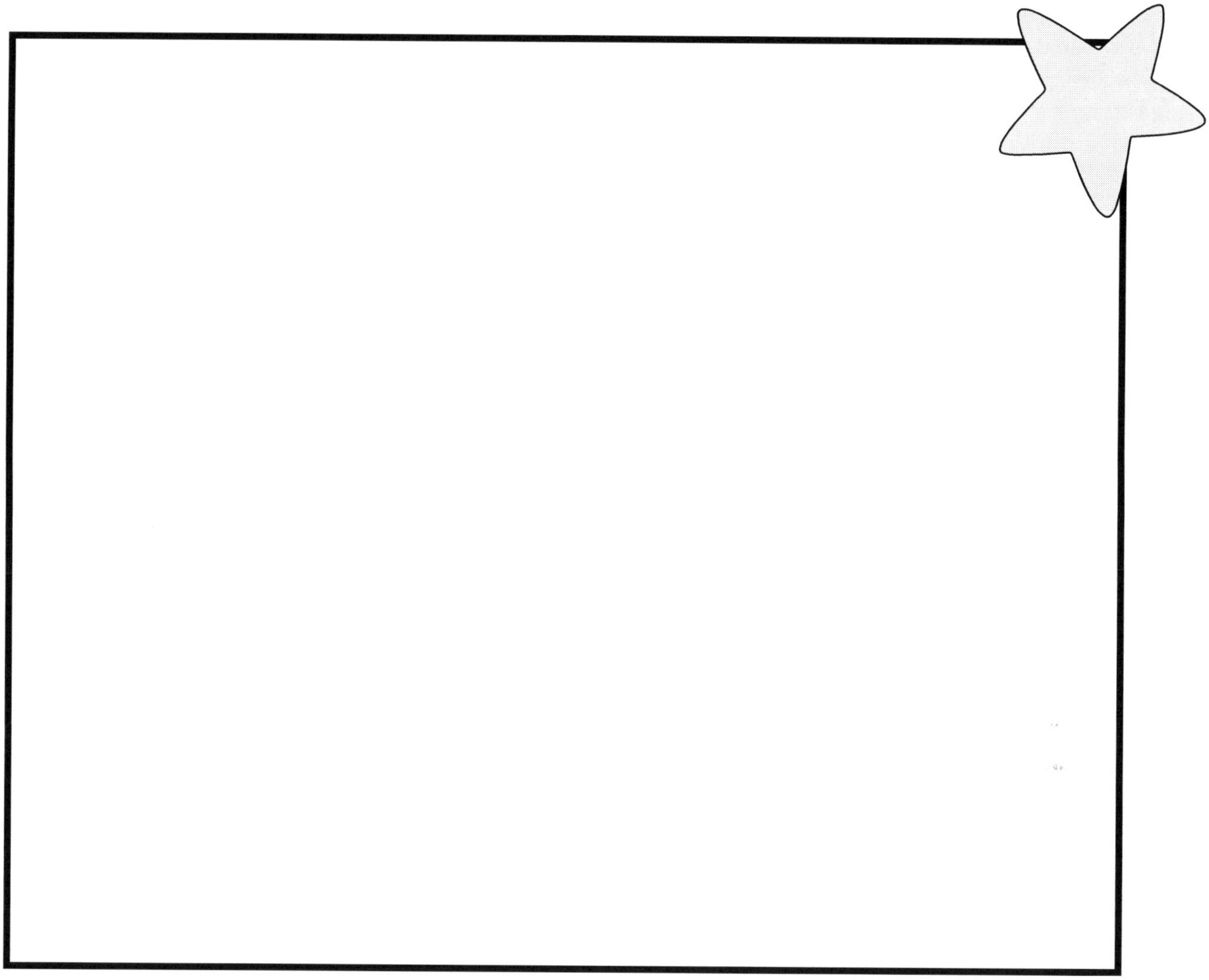

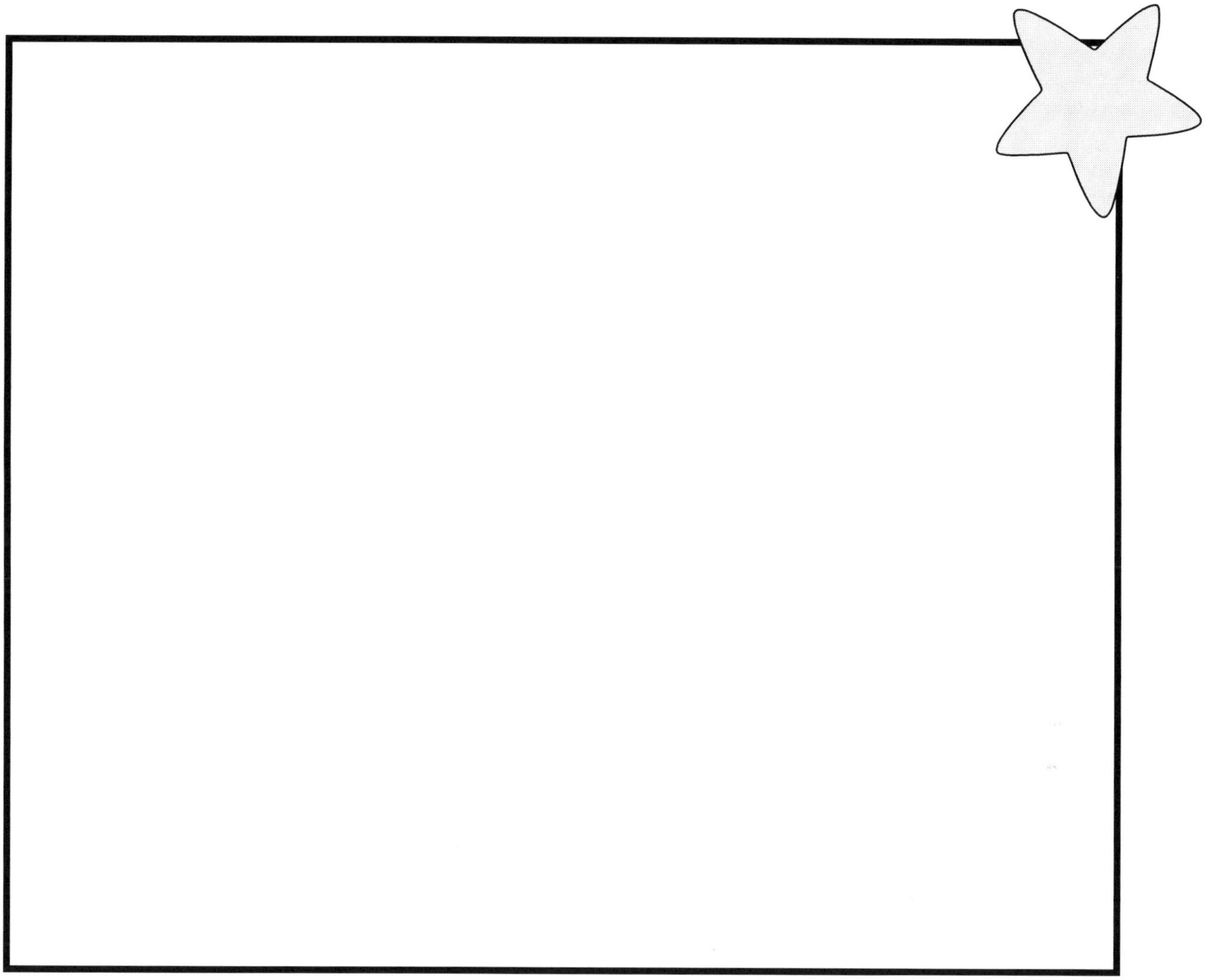

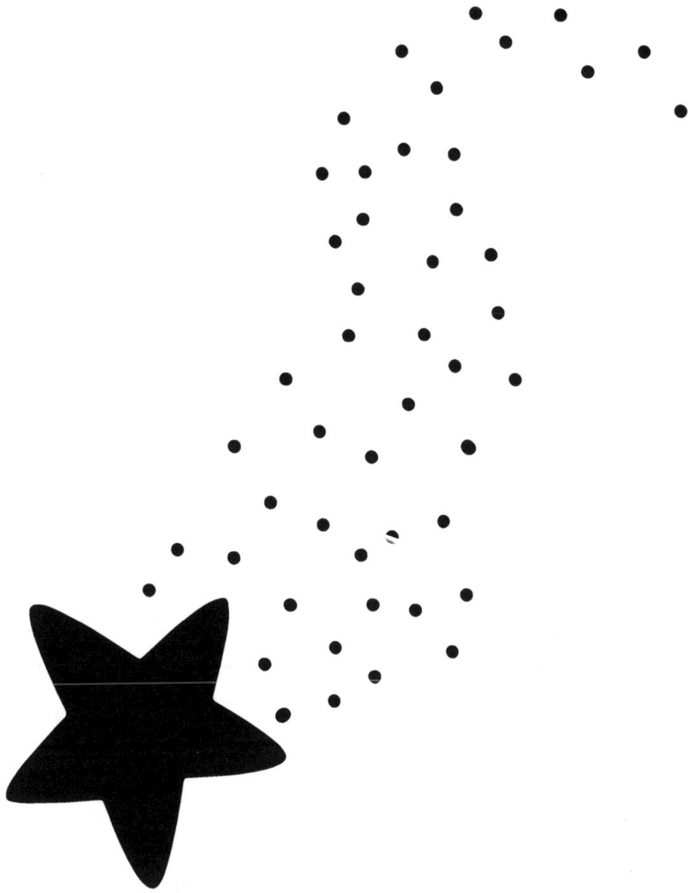

46331765R00062

Made in the USA
Middletown, DE
26 May 2019